LIVING THE *Liturgy*

A Guide to the Lutheran Order of the Divine Service

CARL SCHALK

CONCORDIA PUBLISHING HOUSE · SAINT LOUIS

To the people of
Shepherd of the Lake Lutheran Church
Loudon, Tennessee

A special word of thanks to the Rev. Dr. Paul Grime
for his review and valuable suggestions for this publication.

Published by Concordia Publishing House
3558 S. Jefferson Avenue
St. Louis, MO 63118-3968
1-800-325-3040 • cph.org

Published under the auspices of: Center for Church Music, Concordia University Chicago River Forest, IL 60305-1499.

Manufactured in the United States of America

3 4 5 6 7 8 9 10 31 30 29 28 27 26 25 24 23

Contents

Preface 5

The Origins of the Divine Service 7

How We Got the Divine Service • The Anatomy of Worship • The Church Year

The Divine Service 15

Confession and Absolution

Invocation 17

Confession and Absolution 19

Service of the Word

Entrance, *Kyrie*, Hymn of Praise 21

Salutation and Collect of the Day 22

Scripture Readings 24

Hymn of the Day 27

Sermon 29

Creed 31

Prayer of the Church 33

Exchange of Peace 34

Offering and Offertory 35

Service of the Sacrament

Preface 37

Sanctus 38

Prayer of Thanksgiving 38

Lord's Prayer 39

The Words of Our Lord 39

Pax Domini 39

Agnus Dei 40

Distribution 40

Catechetical Review: The Real Presence of Christ in Holy Communion 42

Post-Communion Canticle 44

Post-Communion Collect 45

Benediction 45

Appendix: History of the Development of the Divine Service 47

Preface

Among the various rites of the Christian Church, at their heart and center is the weekly celebration of the Divine Service (Holy Communion, Eucharist). Mentioned in an early account in the Acts of the Apostles (2:42), we see the beginning of the shape of the celebration that was and is the central act of the Church.

Our understanding of that early description in the Acts of the Apostles is expanded by several early noncanonical descriptions[1] as this rite developed in the Early Church. These developments, in part, were occasioned by changes as the Church ultimately was accepted as legitimate in the Roman Empire and as the Church grew in numbers and prominence in its early centuries. By the early Middle Ages, the basic shape of the Mass had been largely established (see the Appendix). This was the Mass as Luther knew it.

Martin Luther (1483–1546) found much to criticize in the Mass that he had inherited and did not hesitate to correct it where he believed it was in error. But he also saw it as a gift of God and a sign of continuity with the Church. For that reason, he did not abandon the Mass but urged its retention, albeit with corrections. Both Luther's Latin Mass (1523) and his German Mass (1526) clearly reflect his intent to retain the basic shape of the Mass. His German Mass in particular shows the integration of congregational song as a vehicle for singing the liturgy.

In contrast, most of the Reformed sects at the time of the Reformation abandoned the historic structures of the Mass, the Church Year, and the appointed pericopes for each Sunday and

1 Such as *The First Apology of Justin Martyr*, ca. 155, and *The Apostolic Tradition of Hippolytus*, ca. 200.

festival. The result was a worship lacking in richness and depth, cut off from the experience of the Church at worship throughout the centuries and centered almost exclusively around the sermon and the idiosyncrasies of individual leaders.

By the end of the seventeenth century, some Lutherans, influenced by a rising tide of Pietism and the Enlightenment, followed the Reformed tradition down the path of liturgical impoverishment. It would take the nineteenth-century Confessional Revival, a movement begun in Germany and brought to North America by a variety of immigrant groups, to set Lutheranism on the path to recovery. A signal moment in this movement in the United States was the adoption of the Common Service (1888). Based on the "common consent of the best Lutheran orders of the sixteenth century," the Common Service was quickly adopted by virtually all Lutherans in North America and has served as a basic reference for most all later developments.

This little booklet is intended to help all worshipers, young and old, to understand how and why the Divine Service is shaped the way it is. It discusses the intent and meaning of the individual parts and their relation to the whole structure of the service. It can be useful for church musicians and other leaders in worship, worship committees, choir members, and adult education classes as well as new member classes.

This booklet is one way of beginning the conversation about the centrality of worship in the life of the Church.

Carl Schalk (1929–2021)
Distinguished Professor of Church Music
Concordia University Chicago
River Forest, Illinois

The Origins of the Divine Service

How We Got the Divine Service

It may be helpful to begin with an all-too-brief overview of how we got the rite of Holy Communion as currently celebrated among Lutherans. Among the earliest references to worship among early Christians is St. Paul's comment dating from the AD 50s or 60s, even before the Gospels were written:

> And they devoted themselves to the apostles' teaching and the fellowship, to the breaking of bread and the prayers. (Acts 2:42)

This earliest and tantalizingly brief glimpse is expanded in the biblical accounts of the institution of the Lord's Supper in the Synoptic Gospels of Mark (14:22–25), Matthew (26:26–29), and Luke (22:14–20). In these early accounts, we can see the beginnings of a framework that would develop in the years ahead. Other early accounts—such as the *First Apology* of Justin Martyr (ca. 155) and the early third-century *Apostolic Tradition*, often ascribed to Hippolytus of Rome and which included an early Prayer of Thanksgiving—add additional details to this developing history.

By the late fourth century, Christianity was declared a legitimate religion by the Roman government. By the sixth century, the liturgical reforms of St. Gregory (pope from 590–604) had come into being. The basic framework of the Western Catholic Mass was beginning to emerge. By the end of the first millennium the overall shape was clear.

It would be this Mass that—with various additional accretions—would be in use at the time of the sixteenth-century Reformation. This was the Mass that Martin Luther knew and with which he was thoroughly acquainted. It was this order that Luther accepted as a good and gracious gift of God but also one with which he had some serious theological concerns that he set out to address.

It is important to understand that despite Luther's theological disagreements with aspects of the medieval Mass, he argued for retaining its use but correcting it where he understood it to be in error.

> It is not now nor ever has been our intention to abolish the liturgical service of God.[1]
>
> The Mass is held among us and celebrated with the greatest reverence. Nearly all the usual ceremonies are also preserved, except that the parts sung in Latin are interspersed here and there with German hymns.[2]

In both his Latin Mass (1523) and his German Mass (1526), Luther made changes where he believed it was contrary to the Gospel.[3] Apart from those changes, and with a few suggestions based on personal inclinations, he retained the basic shape and structure of the Mass. Luther thus accepted, with the exceptions noted, the basic framework of the Western Mass that he had received.[4]

The Reformed branches of the Reformation took a radically different path. Worship was largely reduced to readings, prayers, and singing restricted to the metrical psalms, all pointing to the central focus of worship, which was the sermon. The Reformed churches essentially abandoned the historic liturgy, the Church Year, and the discipline of appointed lessons. Worship became a sermon-centered event. The sacraments, both Holy Communion—when it was celebrated—and Holy Baptism, generally were understood as symbolic exercises.

---

1 Luther, *Order of Mass and Communion* (1523), AE 53:20.

2 AC XXIV 1.

3 Luther took particular objection to the Canon of the Mass and the Offertory, both of which he excised in his suggested revisions.

4 See Mark Bangert, "Mass," in *Key Words in Church Music* (St. Louis: Concordia Publishing House, 1978), 240–41.

From the later seventeenth and into the nineteenth century much of Lutheranism fell under the influence of Pietism and the Enlightenment. In North America the early Lutheran immigrants of the eighteenth century transplanted their pietistic views and practices to their new homeland. Many Lutherans in the United States, for example, adopted the techniques and practices of revivalism, together with its decision theology, in an attempt to adapt to the cultural situation in a new land.

In reaction, a movement of Confessional Lutheranism arose that sought to reconnect Lutheranism with its historic liturgical and confessional roots, adopting as its signal achievement the Common Service of 1888. This service was based on "the common consent of the best Lutheran orders of the sixteenth century." It was the joint work of the General Synod, the General Council, and the United Synod of the South.

By 1891 the Common Service found its way into the hymnal of the General English Lutheran Conference, and from there into the first English hymnal of The Lutheran Church—Missouri Synod in 1912. It also appeared in the *Common Service Book and Hymnal* (1917), as the liturgy of *The Lutheran Hymnal* (1941) of the Synodical Conference, and in the *Service Book and Hymnal* (1958).

While some modifications in nomenclature have been made by some groups, the Common Service continued to shape the worship of Lutherans throughout the twentieth century and beyond. Its continued presence in most North American Lutheran hymnals bears witness to its enduring influence.

The Anatomy of Worship

The association of the two words *anatomy* and *worship* suggests that worship not only has a discernible structure or shape but also a relationship between the parts of the structure and the whole. This little booklet is an introduction to the structure or anatomy of the central rite of the Western Christian Church—the

Divine Service (Holy Communion, Eucharist)—especially as it is celebrated by Lutherans today.

It is also important to note that while the Divine Service is the central act of the Church's weekly gathering, this celebration does not exist in isolation. The celebration of Holy Communion always occurs within the context of several other structures that help shape its celebration. These include the Church Year, the discipline of appointed readings from Scripture, and the various other rites of the Church that surround and nurture the faith from Baptism to the burial of the dead.

A basic function of this exoskeleton or structure of the rite of Holy Communion is to protect and safeguard that which it encloses. And what it encloses, what it safeguards, is the rich narrative of the story of salvation—the Good News of the Gospel itself in all its richness and depth. There is always the temptation to break into these structures and to turn it to serve other ends.

The components of the rite are not an arbitrary list of items to check off but are instead an intricate web of words and actions that are related to one another, with each one playing a unique role in terms of the whole through a logical progression from one to the next. When the parts of the rite are whimsically rearranged, altered, deleted, or added to, that web is torn apart and the connections are broken.

The Church Year

The Church exists in the world, but it is not of the world. It has a culture and a language all its own. Part of its culture is a unique way of thinking about time. Time, in the Church's view, is linear. It has a beginning and will come to an end. Its trajectory is guided by and celebrates time through the lens of the great narrative of the story of salvation. The framework for that story is the Church Year.

Like most people, the Church celebrates seasons, beginnings and endings, anniversaries, and important events in its life and history. But unlike the secular culture, the Church's celebrations center around the life and work of Jesus Christ and the Church He established. The purpose of the Church Year is to help us rehearse—to "re-hear"—again and again, year in and year out, the story of salvation in all its breadth, depth, and richness.

The Church Year, in its unique way, is both a proclaimer and a teacher of the Gospel. It is a disciplining structure for pastors, church musicians, and congregations alike. It helps us all keep first things first. And we observe and celebrate the Church Year not only on Sundays but every day of the year, day in and day out.

One way of understanding the Church Year is to see it as three large cycles: the Advent—Christmas—Epiphany Cycle (The Time of Christmas); the Lent—Holy Week—Easter Cycle (The Time of Easter); and the Pentecost Cycle (The Time of the Church), dedicated to the Christian life. These cycles might be described as follows:

THE TIME OF CHRISTMAS

ADVENT	CHRISTMAS	EPIPHANY
4 weeks	12 days (December 25–January 6)	Variable, from 1 to 8 weeks

THE TIME OF EASTER

LENT	HOLY WEEK	EASTER
6 weeks (starts on Ash Wednesday)	Palm Sunday–Holy Saturday (includes Maundy Thursday and Good Friday)	7 weeks (a week of weeks, ending on Pentecost)

THE TIME OF THE CHURCH

THE PENTECOST CYCLE		
Begins with Holy Trinity	Variable number of Sundays	Concludes with Last Sunday of the Church Year

As we explore the Church Year more deeply, we discover a rich array of lesser festivals, most relating to the life of Christ. Here are a few of these feasts and festivals together with their appointed dates:

Circumcision and Name of Jesus	January 1
The Purification of Mary and the Presentation of Our Lord	February 2
The Annunciation of Our Lord	March 25
The Visitation	May 31[5]
Mary, Mother of Our Lord	August 15
St. Michael and All Angels	September 29
The Holy Innocents, Martyrs	December 28

We also include a sampling of the days set apart to remember the disciples, apostles, and martyrs, as well as all the saints who have gone before us:

St. Mark, Evangelist	April 25
St. Philip and St. James, Apostles	May 1
The Nativity of St. John the Baptist	June 24
St. Peter and St. Paul, Apostles	June 29
St. Mary Magdalene	July 22
St. Bartholomew, Apostle	August 24
St. Matthew, Apostle and Evangelist	September 21
St. Luke, Evangelist	October 18
All Saints' Day	November 1
St. Andrew, Apostle	November 30
St. Stephen, Martyr	December 26
St. John, Apostle and Evangelist	December 27

In addition are the days set aside as commemorations of others from across the centuries who are remembered for their particular contributions to the life and mission of the Church. These commemorations are listed in the front of every Lutheran hymnbook.[6]

5 This is the date of the feast according to the three-year lectionary. It is observed on July 2 according to the one-year lectionary.

6 For example, see *LSB*, xii–xiii.

Not every congregation will celebrate every feast or festival, saint's day, or commemoration. But congregations should look to the Church Year to broaden their understanding of worship's public witness to the world. Many congregations have yet to begin to explore how these days in the Church Year can enrich their worship.

What could greater attention to the Church Year mean for the public worship life of the Church and its witness to the world? The possibilities are great. The Church Year is not just for Sundays!

The Divine Service

Confession and Absolution

- Invocation
- Confession and Absolution

Service of the Word

- Introit, Psalm, or Entrance Hymn
- *Kyrie* (Lord, Have Mercy)
- Hymn of Praise: *Gloria in Excelsis* (Glory to God in the Highest) or This Is the Feast
- Salutation and Collect of the Day
- Old Testament or First Reading
- Psalm or Gradual
- Epistle or Second Reading
- Alleluia and Verse
- Holy Gospel
- Hymn of the Day
- Sermon
- Creed
- Prayer of the Church
- Exchange of Peace
- Offering and Offertory

Service of the Sacrament

- Preface
- *Sanctus* (Holy, Holy, Holy)
- Prayer of Thanksgiving
- Lord's Prayer
- The Words of Our Lord
- *Pax Domini* (The Peace of the Lord)
- *Agnus Dei* (Lamb of God)
- Distribution
- Post-Communion Canticle
- Post-Communion Collect
- Benediction

Confession and Absolution

Invocation

Worship begins by naming the God we worship. To *invoke* is "to call upon" or "to appeal to." To be sure, God does not come because *we* call, but we have gathered because *He* calls, gathers, enlightens, and sanctifies us. Because God is already present, the invocation is a remembrance of Him placing His name on us in our Baptism. The form of the Invocation is simple and direct. The presiding minister speaks the Invocation:

> Pastor: In the name of the Father and of the ☩ Son and of the Holy Spirit.
> Congregation: Amen.[1]

Having been brought together by the Holy Spirit, the presiding minister announces the name of the God we have gathered to worship. As the presiding minister makes the sign of the cross ☩, the people may follow the presiding minister's example, making the sign of the cross on their forehead or breast in remembrance of their Baptism. And the congregation responds by affirming that confession aloud with their "Amen."

The name of God, for Christians, has always been "Father, Son, and Holy Spirit." The Athanasian Creed proclaims: "The catholic faith is this, that we worship one God in Trinity and Trinity in Unity."[2] That triune God is named in all three ecumenical creeds as "Father, Son, and Holy Spirit," equal in glory, coequal in majesty.

The Athanasian Creed was not written as an idle exercise. It was prepared specifically against heretics (Arius, Apollinaris of

1 *LSB*, 151.

2 *LSB*, 319.

Laodicea, Nestorius) who did not affirm Jesus Christ is true God and true man, God's eternal Son born of the Virgin Mary by the power of the Holy Spirit. The name of God as "Father, Son, and Holy Spirit" is a basic teaching of the Church.

As the Invocation is announced, the people make their affirmation that the Invocation is not simply a pleasant formality or one way to begin worship. Rather, it is affirming a declaration for all the world to hear: "This is the God we worship—the Father, the Son, and the Holy Spirit, one God in three persons."

Many people today, while identifying themselves as "spiritual" or "religious," hesitate to identify themselves as Christian. They may believe in "God," but they cannot say much beyond that. The Invocation announces that we have come to worship not just some kind of god, but the Holy Trinity—Father, Son, and Holy Spirit.

From earliest times the Church has confessed the triune God not only in its creeds but in its songs as well. Ambrose, fourth-century bishop of Milan, concluded many of his hymns with a trinitarian doxology. A favorite hymn from the nineteenth century—"Holy, Holy, Holy" (*LSB* 507)—reflects in its title the triune God whose praise we sing. The final stanza of the eighteenth-century hymn "Holy God, We Praise Thy Name" says it simply and directly:

> Holy Father, holy Son,
>   Holy Spirit, three we name Thee;
> Though in essence only one,
>   Undivided God we claim Thee
> And, adoring, bend the knee
> While we own the mystery. (*LSB* 940:5)

The Holy Trinity is not something we can comprehend intellectually, no matter how hard we may try. It is a mystery. But it is a mystery we claim, a mystery we profess, and a mystery we make our own in our response to the Invocation: "Amen."

Confession and Absolution

In the medieval Church the act of Confession and Absolution was a *private* rite conducted between the penitent and the priest or confessor. It occurred apart from the Mass. Luther, in his Small Catechism (1529), commended private confession and suggested an appropriate wording for its practice. Today, for various reasons, confession and forgiveness is usually practiced as a *corporate* act before Holy Communion. Still, private confession remains a beneficial practice.

Confession begins by acknowledging and giving voice to our absolute inability to redeem ourselves.

> We confess that we are by nature sinful and unclean. We have sinned against You in thought, word, and deed, by what we have done and by what we have left undone.[3]

There is no equivocating. We are captive to sin. It is not just that we do sinful things; we are, in the most basic sense, sinful by our very nature as the result of Adam's fall. In the words of the *New England Horn Book*: "In Adam's fall we sinned all." Luther put it this way: "We are beggars," our hands outstretched for whatever crumbs God will give.[4] We bring nothing to the table.

The first hymn in the first collection of Lutheran hymns printed in 1524 put it this way:

> Fast bound in Satan's chains I lay;
> Death brooded darkly o'er me.
> Sin was my torment night and day;
> In sin my mother bore me.
> But daily deeper still I fell;
> My life became a living hell,
> So firmly sin possessed me. (*LSB* 556:2)

3 *LSB*, 151.

4 See Luther's final written words, *Table Talk* no. 5677 (1546), AE 54:476.

Martin Franzman, a prominent twentieth-century theologian and hymnwriter, put it this way:

> In Adam we have all been one,
>   One huge rebellious man;
> We all have fled that evening voice
>   That sought us as we ran. (*LSB* 569:1)

In Confession we throw ourselves upon the mercy of God. We implore God, for Jesus' sake—who through His suffering, death, and resurrection paid the price for our salvation and won the victory over sin, death, and the devil for us—to grant to us, who cannot save ourselves, mercy and forgiveness.

And having confessed our sin, we hear the comforting words of Absolution or forgiveness, which points ahead to the Sacrament of the Altar later in the liturgy:

> Almighty God in His mercy has given His Son to die for you and for His sake forgives you all your sins. As a called and ordained servant of Christ, and by His authority, I therefore forgive you all your sins in the name of the Father and of the ✠ Son and of the Holy Spirit.[5]

We are declared righteous before God. Yet we are also, in Luther's words, both saint and sinner. That is why we return—week after week—to confess our sin, to receive full and free absolution. And week after week we receive Christ Himself in, with, and under the bread and wine. We receive not just the crumbs that fall from Christ's table but the whole loaf. In the bread and wine of Holy Communion we receive Christ's body and blood, the food that gives us strength for life's journey. That strength, Lutherans believe, is to be found only in Word and Sacrament.

5 *LSB*, 151.

Service of the Word

Entrance, Kyrie, *Hymn of Praise*

The beginning of the Service of the Word may be simple or more elaborate, depending on the liturgical season, the particular feast or festival, or other factors. It may also be shaped by the size of the congregation or the configuration of a particular church building.

Advent and Lent, for example, are liturgical seasons more contemplative in nature and suggest a simpler and more modest beginning. Major feasts, such as Easter, Pentecost, and Christmas, and festivals call for more elaborate celebrations. Three basic elements make up the beginning: an Introit, Psalm, or Entrance Hymn; the *Kyrie* (Lord, Have Mercy); and the Hymn of Praise.

An Introit, Psalm, or Entrance Hymn is sung as those leading worship take their places. In certain liturgical seasons a silent processional led simply by the cross may be appropriate. The singing of a psalm as those leading worship take their places has a long history in Christian worship.[1] Appropriate psalms or passages from psalms may be sung by the congregation, choir, or both in alternation. When a congregational hymn is sung, care should be taken that it does not overwhelm the purpose it is to serve. Such a hymn is not the most important hymn in the service.

The *Kyrie* (Greek for "Lord, have mercy") is the last vestige of the Greek roots of the liturgy and the first of the five great songs of the Divine Service. It is normally sung by the congregation in a litanylike form. On occasion the choir may sing it in the familiar

1 In his German Mass (1526) Luther says, "To begin the service we sing a hymn or a German Psalm in the First [Gregorian] Tone as follows," and then gives a musical example of how the Psalm would be sung (AE 53:70–71, quote on p. 69).

three-, six-, ninefold, or litany forms, or as a motet. A chorale paraphrase of the *Kyrie* to be sung by the congregation has gained wider use in recent years ("Kyrie! God, Father," *LSB* 942.) Each of these options has precedence in Lutheran liturgical and musical practice.

The Hymn of Praise, or *Gloria in Excelsis* (Latin for "Glory in the highest"), is the song of the angels at the birth of Christ (Luke 2:14). Historically, it is sung weekly—except in Advent and Lent when it is omitted. Its present, expanded form was established as early as the fourth century. It is the second of the five great songs of the Divine Service. A recent Hymn of Praise, "This Is the Feast," has gained wide acceptance and is appointed for the Easter season and several lesser festivals. A hymn paraphrase of the *Gloria in Excelsis*, "All Glory Be to God on High" (*LSB* 947), ascribed to Nicolaus Decius from the sixteenth century, is also widely used.

In Lutheran practice the choice among these various options should reflect the character of the liturgical season or festival. Carefully chosen, they can bring a richness and depth to worship. They are not options to be randomly used in pursuit of "variety."

The beginning of the Service of the Word prepares us for the two central focal points of the Sunday celebration: hearing the proclamation of the Word and celebrating Holy Communion.

Salutation and Collect of the Day

The Collect (Prayer) of the Day announces the central theme of each Sunday, feast, or festival, which is enlarged upon in the readings from Scripture that immediately follow. The Collect of the Day is part of the Proper of the liturgy, that is, it is "proper" or varies according to the specific Sunday, feast, or festival in which it occurs.

In the Western Church each Collect of the Day is marked by two important characteristics. The first is its brevity. These prayers say what they intend as simply and in as few words as is necessary. The second characteristic is its unique form. Here is an example of both the brevity and succinctness of the Collect of the Day:

> Almighty and everlasting God, You despise nothing You have made and forgive the sins of all who are penitent. Create in us new and contrite hearts that lamenting our sins and acknowledging our wretchedness we may receive from You full pardon and forgiveness; through Jesus Christ, Your Son, our Lord, who lives and reigns with You and the Holy Spirit, one God, now and forever.[2]

Note the fivefold shape: (1) the announcement to whom the prayer is addressed, (2) a description of what God has done, (3) what we pray for in this prayer, (4) the desired benefit, and (5) in whose name we pray. In the Western tradition, the Church's prayers, with few exceptions, are addressed to the Father, through the Son, in the Holy Spirit.

The address	Almighty and everlasting God,
What God has done	You despise nothing You have made and forgive the sins of all who are penitent.
What we now pray for	Create in us new and contrite hearts
The desired benefit	that lamenting our sins and acknowledging our wretchedness we may receive from You full pardon and forgiveness
The name in which we pray	through Jesus Christ, Your Son, our Lord, who lives and reigns with You and the Holy Spirit, one God, now and forever.

All respond with "Amen," affirming their assent to this prayer.

The Collect of the Day—as with the Prayer of the Church discussed later—is part of the public worship and witness of the Church. Both prayers speak clearly and carefully, avoiding the

2 Collect of the Day for Ash Wednesday, in *LSB Propers of the Day*, 26.

pitfalls of a superficial spontaneity. First and foremost, they are the *Church's* prayers.

The Collect of the Day sets the context for the themes of the readings from Scripture that follow.

Old Testament or First Reading

The first of the two central focal points of worship in the Western Church is the proclaiming of the Word of God. There are three readings from Holy Scripture appointed for each Sunday and festival: the Old Testament or First Reading, the Epistle or Second Reading, and the Holy Gospel.

The Old Testament reading rehearses the story of how God acted to save His people in Old Testament times. Throughout the year worshipers hear the great stories of the creation of the world, the fall of humanity, the flood, the captivity in Egypt, and the rescue of God's chosen people from the hand of Pharaoh. We hear readings from the Books of Moses, from the historical books of the Old Testament, as well as the prophets' heralding of the news of what God has done to save His chosen people in the past and what God promises yet to do.

As New Testament Christians, we hear the message of the Old Testament from the perspective of the New Testament. We hear the history of Israel through New Testament ears. We see the Old Testament prophecies as fulfilled in the New Testament. As one listens attentively to the Old Testament reading, one discovers how often it connects with the later Gospel reading. To hear regularly the Old Testament stories of how God saved His people in the past is to connect us with what is, in fact, part of *our* story. It is a story as relevant today as when it was first heard—an old story now heard with new ears.

For some days in the Church Year, the appointed reading comes from either the Book of Acts or Revelation. When this is the case, the text is presented as "the First Reading from," citing the book.

At the conclusion of the Old Testament or First Reading the lector says simply: "This is the Word of the Lord." And the congregation responds with its assent: "Thanks be to God."

Psalm or Gradual

Before proceeding to the Epistle or Second Reading, the congregation responds to the Old Testament reading by praising God with the songs of praise, lament, instruction, encouragement, and comfort found in the Old Testament Book of Psalms (literally, "Book of Praises"). Recent Lutheran hymnbooks include a number of simple melodic formulas for singing the Psalms. They are easily learned, and many congregations sing the Psalms in this way.

As contemporary Christians, we see and hear the Old Testament through the prism of the New Testament. Christian practice adds a trinitarian doxology:

> Glory be to the Father and to the Son
>   and to the Holy Spirit;
> as it was in the beginning,
>   is now, and will be forever. Amen.

Epistle or Second Reading

The Second Reading, traditionally referred to as the Epistle, is a reading taken from the epistles (from the Greek *epistole*, "letter") written to various Christian congregations or individuals in the Early Church. These letters usually address specific concerns or problems. The apostle Paul wrote thirteen epistles. Other authors include Peter, James, John, and Jude.

A reference in the second-century writing of Justin Martyr mentions that the early Christians would gather on Sunday to listen to "the memoirs of the apostles or the writings of the prophets."[3] It

3 *First Apology*, 67.

is difficult for us today to realize the rapt attention that the early Christians brought to hearing the reading of these letters. Their origins suggest that these epistles were written largely for purposes of instruction. They serve us today with a similar purpose.

For some days in the Church Year, the appointed reading comes from either the Book of Acts or Revelation. When this is the case, the text is presented as "the Second Reading from," citing the book.

The Epistle or Second Reading is introduced in similar fashion to the Old Testament or First Reading. The lector announces: "The Epistle is from . . ." with the name of the book and the chapter following. At the conclusion of the reading, the lector says, "This is the Word of the Lord." The congregation responds: "Thanks be to God."

Alleluia and Verse

Following the Epistle or Second Reading, the choir or congregation sings the Alleluia and Verse in preparation to hear the reading of the Holy Gospel.[4] The reading of the Gospel is the climax of the three readings in the Service of the Word. It is important that the Alleluia and Verse, by its length and character, not overwhelm the Gospel that follows. The congregation stands as a sign of respect as it listens attentively to the reading.

Holy Gospel

On particularly important Sundays, feasts (such as Easter, Pentecost, or Christmas), or festivals, there may be a Gospel procession into the center of the congregation where the Holy Gospel is then read from the midst of the assembly. Such a procession may involve a crucifer, the Gospel book bearer, candle bearers, and the one who is to read the Gospel.

---

4 During the Lenten season, the Alleluia is omitted and the words of Joel 2:13 are sung instead; see *LSB*, 157.

The Old Testament and Epistle may be read by assisting lay ministers called lectors. The reading of the Holy Gospel, however, is usually read by the one who is preaching since the sermon is normally based on the Gospel reading. Following the announcement of the Holy Gospel, the congregation responds with the acclamation: "Glory to You, O Lord." At the conclusion of the reading, the assembly says, "Praise to You, O Christ." The Hymn of the Day follows.

The reading of Holy Scripture in the public worship of the Church is a high and holy privilege. It involves careful preparation, familiarity with the content of the reading, and attention to aspects of public speaking. Many congregations train lectors so they can fulfill their role more effectively. To do any less is to misunderstand the importance of the role of those who read in the public worship of the Church and, unintentionally, to disrespect those who listen.

Hymn of the Day

The Hymn of the Day—or the *de tempore* hymn—is an appointed Proper, that is, it varies according to the Sunday, feast, and festival. It is the chief hymn of the service. Its content is related to the broad themes of the liturgical season and the Scripture readings for the day, especially the Gospel. Its purpose is, in Luther's words, to "Proclaim the wonders God has done, How His right arm the vict'ry won" (*LSB* 556:1). This hymn is sung immediately before the sermon.

The practice of associating a specific hymn with a particular Sunday, feast, or festival predates the Reformation.[5] Hymns such as the eighth-century *Gloria, laus et honor tibi* ("All Glory, Laud, and Honor," *LSB* 442), the sixth-century *Pange lingua gloriosi* ("Sing, My Tongue, the Glorious Battle," *LSB* 454), or the ninth-century *Veni,*

5 For a more detailed account, see Carl Schalk, *The Hymn of the Day and Its Use in Lutheran Worship* (St. Louis: Concordia Publishing House, 1983).

Creator Spiritus ("Come, Holy Ghost, Creator Blest," *LSB* 498/499) had become associated with Palm Sunday, Good Friday, and the Rite of Ordination, respectively, long before the Reformation.

The Reformation Church built and expanded this earlier practice, gradually establishing through common consent a hymn for each Sunday of the Church Year. Two early examples of hymns that quickly became widely established in the early Reformation as *de tempore* hymns were Martin Luther's German version of the fourth-century *Veni redemptor gentium* ("Savior of the Nations, Come," *LSB* 332) for the First Sunday in Advent and "Christ Jesus Lay in Death's Strong Bands" (*LSB* 458, a text written by Luther) for the Resurrection of Our Lord. These hymns were soon joined by Philipp Nicolai's "Wake, Awake, for Night Is Flying" (*LSB* 516) for the Last Sunday of the Church Year and "O Morning Star, How Fair and Bright" (*LSB* 395) for Epiphany. By the early eighteenth century this practice had become widely established, many congregations including lists of these *de tempore* hymns in their church orders or constitutions.

By the late seventeenth and the early eighteenth century, however, many Lutheran churches, as a result of the influence of Pietism and the Enlightenment, had abandoned the Church Year, the use of appointed lessons, the use of the *de tempore* hymn, and the liturgical tradition of the Church in general. What was left was the sermon, surrounded by a few prayers and hymns. Luther Reed, the most important North American Lutheran liturgical scholar of the first part of the twentieth century, describes the situation as follows:

> The idea of choosing the hymn entirely with reference to the Sermon dates from the early eighteenth century. After this time the Sermon more and more dominated the service. During the next hundred years,

> with increasing indifference to the church year, it [the Sermon] ruled the liturgy and the hymns.[6]

The Hymn of the Day (*de tempore* hymn) had become the "sermon hymn." It would take the Confessional Revival of the nineteenth century to begin to change that mistaken understanding.

Today the designation "Hymn of the Day" is commonly used among Lutherans, and lists can be found in most Lutheran hymnbooks. These lists reflect changes and accommodations made over time in response to a variety of factors.

The Hymn of the Day is both a proclaimer of the Gospel and, simultaneously, a teacher. The regular and recurrent use of these appointed hymns helps impress their texts and tunes on the minds and hearts of those who sing them. Their strong theology, coupled with robust and sturdy tunes, is a tribute to their persistent use and popularity among Lutherans.

The Hymn of the Day is grounded in Scripture, directly related to the liturgical season or feast or festival, and reflects the themes of the appointed lessons. What the Hymn of the Day is *not* is a "sermon hymn."

The Hymn of the Day is a uniquely Lutheran contribution to the Church's song. Lutherans believe that the Good News of the Gospel should sound out with equal clarity, vigor, and theological integrity not only from the pulpit but from the song of the congregation as well. The Hymn of the Day is an important vehicle toward that end.

Sermon

One of the significant contributions of the Lutheran Reformation was to restore preaching to a place of greater prominence than it had held in the centuries prior to the Reformation.

6 Luther D. Reed, *The Lutheran Liturgy: A Study of the Common Liturgy of the Lutheran Church in America*, rev. ed. (Philadelphia: Muhlenberg Press, 1947), 305.

The Sermon is part of the Service of the Word, as Holy Scripture is read, proclaimed, and explicated.

The role of the sermon was for Luther not only to make clear the utter helplessness of all humanity before a righteous God but to proclaim the Good News of salvation through the atoning work of Jesus Christ, God's Son, for the sins of the world. Lutherans emphasize the preaching of both Law and Gospel: the Law to show us our sin, and the Gospel as the remedy in the life, death, and resurrection of Jesus Christ. In the often-repeated comment attributed to Reinhold Niebuhr (1882–1971), the sermon is to "comfort the afflicted and to afflict the comfortable."

To preach only the Law leaves the hearer without hope. To preach only a gauzy "Good News" is to avoid confronting the hearer with the enormity of our sinful nature. Such preaching too easily slips into what Dietrich Bonhoeffer called "cheap grace." That is why faithful preaching involves study, reading, contemplation, prayer, and a careful and faithful application of the texts to the immediate circumstances.

Disciplined by the Church Year and the appointed readings for the day, the appointed Gospel takes pride of place in sermon preparation. Luther, in his German Mass (1526), suggested that it was the Gospel reading that should be the basis of the sermon on every Sunday.

John Donne, the sixteenth-century poet, in his "Hymn to God, My God, in My Sickness," expresses it in this way:

> So, in his purple wrapp'd, receive me, Lord;
> By these his thorns, give me his other crown;
> And as to others' souls I preach'd thy word,
> Be this my text, my sermon to mine own:
> "Therefore that he may raise, the Lord throws down."

That is a reminder that we are all sick, sick unto death. But it also reminds us that in Christ's crown of thorns we are given that greater crown of life eternal; that, like Christ, before we can be raised up, we must be cast down.

Preaching is about reminding us of that simple fact and helping us all to move from the hopeless accusation of the Law to the sure and certain promise of the Gospel.

Creed

A creed, the dictionary reminds us, is "a brief, authoritative statement of belief."[7] By the end of the fifth century, three Christian creeds had emerged: the Apostles' Creed, the Nicene-Constantinopolitan Creed, and the Confession of Athanasius or, as it is more simply referred to, the Athanasian Creed. They are usually referred to as the three "ecumenical creeds," so called because they were agreed to and accepted as authoritative by the entire Christian Church at that time.

The earliest to emerge was the Apostles' Creed, used in the Early Church at the sacrament of Christian initiation, Holy Baptism. The second was the Nicene or Nicene-Constantinopolitan Creed (325/381), traditionally used at the Divine Service. The third, or Athanasian Creed, is the longest of the creeds and is associated with Trinity Sunday. Based on the teachings of Athanasius (296–373), bishop of Alexandria, it was written after his lifetime.

These three creeds appear at the beginning of the Book of Concord, the confessional writings of the Lutheran Church. Their pride of place and their affirmation in the Book of Concord is testimony to the fact that Lutheranism, from the beginning, sees itself as a reforming movement within the whole Church. The early Lutherans never sought to divorce themselves from the continuity of Christ's Church, nor do we seek this today. Every Lutheran pastor subscribes to these creeds at the time of ordination.

7 William D. Lewis and Edgar A. Singer, eds., *The Winston Simplified Dictionary* (Philadelphia: John C. Winston, 1919), s.v. "Creed."

Having heard the Word proclaimed in the readings from Holy Scripture, sung in the Hymn of the Day, and meditated on in the Sermon, the Creed is now confessed by the congregation—affirming it not only individually but also collectively—as the faith of the Church.

The Nicene Creed is structured in three distinct parts, one for each of the three persons of the Holy Trinity. This creed came into being to clarify what the Church of the fourth century believed about the nature of Christ and the Holy Trinity. It was prompted by the teachings of Arius (256–335) of Alexandria, Egypt. Arius held that Christ, the Second Person of the Trinity, was not God because He was not eternal. Phrases in the Nicene Creed describing Christ as "God of God, Light of Light, very God of very God, begotten, not made, being of one substance with the Father" underscore the equality of the three Persons of the Trinity and the Church's rejection of the teachings of Arius and various other heretical views.

The Athanasian Creed underscores the central importance of the Trinity when it confesses: "Whoever desires to be saved must, above all, hold the catholic faith. . . . And the catholic faith is this, that we worship one God in Trinity and Trinity in Unity."[8] Arius's heretical views are not just some ancient theological controversy. Whenever we hear someone speaking of Jesus Christ as simply a great teacher, an important prophet, or a great moral example, we are hearing modern echoes of an ancient heresy.

When we come together to worship, we come to confess the faith we hold, the faith of the Christian Church. We confess that faith to God, to one another, and to the world. As we confess, we remind God (and ourselves) of the promises made to our fathers, we build up one another in the faith, and we proclaim our faith and praise to those who hear our confession.

8 *LSB*, 319.

Prayer of the Church

The Prayer of the Church is not a haphazard collection of petitions thrown together by whatever may have caught the attention of the one leading the prayers. It has a general design and shape, a unique anatomy all its own. The introduction of the prayer gives us a clue:

> Let us pray for the whole Church of God in Christ Jesus
> and for all people according to their needs.[9]

The traditional template for the Prayer of the Church provides petitions for:

1. The whole Church
2. The nations
3. Those in need
4. The congregation
5. Special needs

In general, the petitions begin with the broader view, gradually narrowing to the particular needs and concerns of the local congregation. It is salutary to be reminded, week after week, that the scope of our prayer as people of God is always broader than the immediate concerns of the particular congregation.

The Prayer of the Church is a unifying element in the Church's worship. For example, in the Prayer of the Church we pray for good government and wise leadership, not for particular political parties. Likewise, in praying for the sick, we do not demand that God heal this person or else. Rather, we pray that God's will be done.

In the Early Church, the Prayer of the Church was ordinarily led by the deacon because the deacon was directly responsible for addressing the specific needs of members of the local church. In the past the Prayer of the Church, or "General Prayer" as it was often called, was a lengthy monologue by the presiding minister. Today the Prayer of the Church, in a litanylike form, may be led by

9 *LSB Altar Book*, 142.

an assisting minister. Each petition concludes with "Lord, in Your mercy" or a similar phrase, and the congregation responds with "Hear our prayer."

In many congregations those leading the Prayer of the Church have been encouraged to write their own prayers rather than using as models the historic prayers of the Church. Care must be taken that the Prayer of the Church does not become simply the prayer of an individual, a bulletin board of congregational events, a way of reminding the listeners of the chief points of the sermon, nor an opportunity to give vent to personal social, political, or religious views. This prayer, we need reminding, is the Prayer *of the Church*.

All prayer is ultimately a way of shaping our will to that of our Creator and Redeemer, not a way of bending God's will to ours. Prayer is not simply asking for things. The conclusion to the Prayer of the Church is a reminder that all is finally in God's hands:

> Into Your hands, O Lord, we commend all for whom we pray, trusting in Your mercy; through Your Son, Jesus Christ, our Lord.[10]

To which the congregation responds: "Amen."

Exchange of Peace

The Exchange of Peace, earlier in its history, was referred to as the Kiss of Peace. The apostle Paul frequently concluded his epistles with the instruction to greet one another with a holy kiss (see, for example, Romans 16:16; 1 Corinthians 16:20). Historically, it was shared in the service just prior to the Service of the Sacrament.

The Exchange of Peace and the Offering are intimately connected. Matthew 5:23–24 says it this way:

> So if you are offering your gift at the altar and there remember that your brother [or sister] has something against you, leave your gift there before the altar and

10 *LSB Altar Book*, 142.

> go. First be reconciled to your brother, and then come and offer your gift.

This is a description of the Exchange of Peace as—first and foremost—an act of reconciliation. In most congregations today, members grasp hands and say to each other: "The peace of the Lord be with you." This act is a profound sign of reconciling what before was unreconciled. It is a mutual act of asking for and receiving forgiveness.

What this exchange is *not* is a friendly moment to say, "Hello, how are you?" to visitors or someone you have not seen for a while. Nor is it a time to say, "Glad to see you in church." It is a moment to celebrate God's forgiveness and share the peace it brings.

Offering and Offertory

Now with hearts forgiven, with neighbors reconciled, with a clean heart and renewed with a right spirit within, we can offer our gifts. While many think of the gathering of the gifts as only monetary gifts, some congregations also bring forward the bread and wine, the gifts needed for Holy Communion. On some occasions, congregations make provision for people to bring forward gifts of food, clothing, or other items gathered for distribution to those in need.

As the gifts are brought forward, the Offertory is sung. It is a song of thanksgiving for these gifts given and received. Historically, the Offertory was a Proper text from the psalms that changed from week to week. More typically now among Lutherans the congregation sings a psalm such as "What shall I render to the Lord?" (Psalm 116:12–13, 17–19) or "Create in me a clean heart, O God" (Psalm 51:10–12). Our offering, as individuals or as a congregation, is a reflection of the total offering of all that we have and are, a symbol of the total giving of ourselves. How might we as individuals or as a congregation understand this moment and use that understanding for Christlike action? That question is worthy of a congregation's time and attention.

But whatever our gifts, large or small, ones that command attention or, like the widow's mite, go unnoticed, God accepts them from a forgiven and forgiving heart "for the sake of him who offered himself for us, Jesus Christ, our Lord."[11]

11 *LBW*, 67.

Service of the Sacrament

Preface

The Preface begins with three brief exchanges that date to the beginning of the third century:

> **Pastor**: The Lord be with you.
> **Congregation**: And also with you.
>
> **Pastor**: Lift up your hearts.
> **Congregation**: We lift them to the Lord.
>
> **Pastor**: Let us give thanks to the Lord our God.
> **Congregation**: It is right to give Him thanks and praise.[1]

The Proper Preface then continues as the pastor leads the congregation in giving thanks for the Lord's goodness: "It is truly good, right, and salutary that we should at all times and in all places give thanks to You."[2] It is from this exuberant giving of thanks that one of the names for the Sacrament comes: the Eucharist.

The Proper Preface goes on to proclaim the saving work of God through His beloved Son, focusing on different themes with the changing seasons of the Church Year. It concludes with a grand invitation to join with the whole heavenly host in singing our adoration of the God of our salvation: "Therefore with angels and archangels and with all the company of heaven, we laud and magnify Your glorious name, evermore praising You and saying . . ."[3]

1 *LSB*, 160.

2 *LSB*, 161.

3 *LSB*, 161.

Sanctus

Then follows the *Sanctus* ("Holy, Holy, Holy"), the fourth great song of the Divine Service that is sung by the congregation. Drawn from the song of the angels that Isaiah heard in his vision (Isaiah 6:3), we join our voices in the unending praise that attends to our holy God in the heavenly places. With "angels and archangels" we acknowledge that we are in the very presence of the God who comes to save us ("Hosanna"). Also placed on our lips are the words from Matthew 21:9 with which Jesus was greeted during His triumphal entry into Jerusalem ("Blessed is He who comes in the name of the Lord"). This is a confession of what we believe is happening in this service—that Jesus, God's own Son, is coming among us with blessing and life.

Prayer of Thanksgiving

In the earliest centuries of the Church, Christians developed various patterns of prayer that surrounded the Lord's own Words of Institution. In the centuries before the Reformation, however, these prayers had accumulated many additions that Luther felt reeked of works-righteousness. As a result, in his Latin Mass (1523) and his German Mass (1526), Luther excised all these prayers, leaving only the Words of Institution. While acknowledging that Luther's concern was justified, more recent generations of Lutheran liturgical scholars have looked back to the Early Church for more appropriate models of this prayer. As a result, eucharistic prayers, in a variety of forms, have been reintroduced for use among North American Lutherans since the middle of the twentieth century.

What must remain at the heart of any prayer that we offer is faithfulness to the Lord's own institution. Thus, most naturally, we continue the theme of the Preface, where thanksgiving to God is given, following Jesus' own practice ("and when He had given thanks . . ."). We do this by recounting God's saving deeds. He is the one who not only created us but also sent His "only-begotten Son into our flesh to bear our sin and be our Savior." And so we petition this gracious God to "forgive, renew, and strengthen us."[4] Bound together with Christ in this sacred meal, we pray that God would join us with all the faithful to give our unending thanks and praise.

Lord's Prayer

As God's people prepare to receive their Lord, they take up the prayer that He has taught us to pray, the Our Father. This is the Church's table prayer, which in the earliest centuries of the Church Christians were instructed to pray three times a day—morning, noon, and night. Luther also instructs us in the Small Catechism to pray it when rising each morning and before going to bed each night.

As God's people gather to receive the Lord's body and blood, there is no more fit prayer. Our prayer for daily bread is fulfilled in this setting as we receive the very bread of life. Likewise, we pray for forgiveness, confident that in this Sacrament we receive not only forgiveness but also life and salvation. Fortified by Christ's body and blood, we can commend ourselves to the will of God and confidently trust that He will deliver us from all evil.

The Words of Our Lord

Without the words with which Jesus instituted His Holy Supper our actions would be worthless. But because He has said it—"This is My body . . . This is My blood"—we know it is true, whatever our senses or reason would say to the contrary. But our Lord tells us more—not only what it is but what it is for: the forgiveness of sins. And who it is for: you!

Pax Domini

As the communicants prepare to come forward to receive their Lord's gift of life, a blessing is now spoken over them: "The peace

4 *LSB*, 161.

of the Lord be with you always."[5] In his liturgical reforms, Luther reinterpreted this ancient formula, shifting it from another liturgical greeting to a powerful proclamation of forgiveness. And with it, another benefit of the Sacrament is introduced in the service, for with forgiveness of sins comes peace with God. With such a blessing, the congregation can only give its heartfelt assent: "Amen."

Agnus Dei

The fifth of the great songs of the Divine Service is now sung: "Lamb of God, You take away the sin of the world." Here we address Jesus specifically, an acknowledgment that He is now here present in His body and blood for our forgiveness. This is the Paschal Lamb who died in place of the firstborn before the exodus (Exodus 12). This is the suffering Lamb who bore our iniquities and carried our sorrows (Isaiah 53). We make our fervent cry three times, praying twice for mercy, and then for peace. We are now ready to receive the One who has come to bring us life.

Distribution

The consecrated elements of bread and wine—the body and blood of Christ—are now ready to be received by the communicants. The presiding minister first administers the consecrated bread as a sign of admission to the Sacrament of Holy Communion. The wine may be administered by assisting ministers. When the bread is administered, the presiding minister says, "The body of Christ" or "The body of Christ given for you." As the cup is administered the assisting minister says, "The blood of Christ" or "The blood of Christ for you." As the communicants receive the bread and wine, they may make the sign of the cross ☩ and respond "Amen."

Traditionally the communicants kneeled at the altar rail to receive the elements. More recently, many congregations have adopted a continuous or processional style in which the communicants

5 *LSB*, 163.

receive the elements at the foot of the chancel while standing. Some congregations use intinction, in which the bread is dipped into the chalice and then taken into the mouth by the communicant. Some of these details will vary to accommodate particular church buildings as well as the number of people communing.

Luther suggested that the congregation sing hymns in connection with Holy Communion and during the distribution of the elements. He suggested some specific chorales he thought particularly appropriate. They included his own *Sanctus*, "Isaiah, Mighty Seer in Days of Old" (*LSB* 960); John Hus's "Jesus Christ, Our Blessed Savior" (*LSB* 627); "O Lord, We Praise Thee" (*LSB* 617, Luther added two stanzas to this medieval hymn); and Nicolaus Decius's "Lamb of God, Pure and Holy" (*LSB* 434). *Lutheran Service Book* contains a wide selection of Communion hymns.

Envision this scenario: as the distribution of the elements begins, observe a period of silence. Allow time for the congregation to ponder the wonder of the sound of the communicants approaching the Table of the Lord. The wonder of young and old, fit and frail, friends or strangers we have yet to meet, all making their way to receive the body and blood of their Lord and Savior for "the forgiveness of sin, life, and salvation."

Then sing a carefully chosen hymn. Sing all the stanzas, perhaps alternating between congregation and choir or men and women. Allow time for quiet meditation and prayer for congregants to ponder quietly what they have just sung, what they have observed, and what they have received in Holy Communion.

Then with the Distribution complete, we are ready to respond in thanks and praise in the Post-Communion Canticle as the Table is cleared.

Catechetical Review: The Real Presence of Christ in Holy Communion

The two central focal points of the Sunday liturgy are the Word and the Sacrament of Holy Communion, or as Robert Jenson names them, the audible Word and the visible Word—the Word we hear with our ears and the Word we see, touch, and taste in the bread and wine.

Lutherans believe that Christ is truly present for us in the bread and wine of Holy Communion. It is a "real" presence; Christ is truly present *in, with, and under* the bread and wine. That is, Christ's presence is a mystery that we cannot explain by human reason. It is a matter of faith.

This is why Lutherans handle the consecrated elements with appropriate care, reverence, and respect. Thus any consecrated bread remaining at the conclusion of the rite is normally consumed by the presiding and assisting ministers. Any consecrated wine remaining is usually either consumed by the presiding minister, poured down a special stone basin that drains directly into the earth, or is poured directly into the ground from which it came. In many congregations, some of the consecrated bread and wine is set aside to be taken to those of the community who, because of sickness, frailty, or other circumstances, could not be at the Sunday celebration.

Throughout history others have sought to reconcile this mystery of Christ's presence in the Sacrament with human reason. Among the Reformed theologians of the sixteenth century, Ulrich Zwingli, at the Marburg Colloquy of 1529, explained that Holy Communion is nothing more than a simple, symbolic, memorial meal. The Roman Catholic Church, employing terms from Greek philosophy, explains that the *substance* or *essence* of the bread and wine in Holy Communion are changed into Christ's body and blood while retaining their outward appearance, or *accidents*, of bread and wine. This is referred to as *transubstantiation*. The Anglican Church in the *Book of Common Prayer* of Edward VI (1552) stated that Christ's presence in the bread and wine, if there at all, must be understood as some kind of "spiritual" presence. They explained in the so-called "Black Rubric" that

> as concerning the natural body and blood of our Saviour Christ, they are in heaven and not here. For it is against the truth of Christ's true natural body, to be in more places than in one at one time.[6]

Luther's understanding of Christ's presence in the bread and wine of Holy Communion was unequivocal. Christ's body and blood are truly present for us in Holy Communion. They are for us to eat and to drink for the forgiveness of our sins, for life, and for our salvation.

As God provided food and drink for His people Israel in the wilderness, so God provides food and drink for our journey here in this life. In Luther's famous Communion hymn, which he reworked from a fifteenth-century text, he set forth his belief:

> O Lord, we praise Thee, bless Thee, and adore Thee,
> In thanksgiving bow before Thee.
> Thou with Thy body and Thy blood didst nourish
> Our weak souls that they may flourish:
> O Lord, have mercy!
> May Thy body, Lord, born of Mary,
> That our sins and sorrows did carry,
> And Thy blood for us plead
> In all trial, fear, and need:
> O Lord, have mercy! (*LSB* 617:1)

As we in faith receive the bread and wine and as we hear the words "The body of Christ" and "The blood of Christ—for you," may we believe it and accept it as the mystery it is.

And rejoice!

---

6 Bard Thompson, *Liturgies of the Western Church* (Cleveland: World Publishing, 1961), 284.

Post-Communion Canticle

Having received the body and blood of Christ in Holy Communion, the response of the congregation is that of thanksgiving for this gift of the forgiveness of sins, life, and salvation. The traditional canticle among Lutherans has been the *Nunc Dimittis*, Simeon's song of praise in the temple at having seen the Savior of the world.

> Lord, now You let Your servant go in peace; Your word has been fulfilled. My own eyes have seen the salvation which You have prepared in the sight of ev'ry people: A light to reveal You to the nations and the glory of Your people Israel.[7]

This canticle, one of the so-called "Lukan psalms," concludes with the trinitarian Lesser Gloria. The singing of the canticle occurs as the Table is being cleared. Luther wrote a hymn paraphrase of the *Nunc Dimittis*, "In Peace and Joy I Now Depart" (*LSB* 938), which may be used as an option for the prose canticle.

A second Post-Communion Canticle that has found wide acceptance among Lutherans in recent years is "Thank the Lord":

> Thank the Lord and sing His praise; tell ev'ryone what He has done. Let all who seek the Lord rejoice and proudly bear His name. He recalls His promises and leads His people forth in joy with shouts of thanksgiving. Alleluia, alleluia.[8]

The musical settings of these canticles reflect both the solemnity and the joy of this moment. Having touched and tasted how good the Lord is in giving Himself to us in Holy Communion, we go forth to "tell everyone what He has done," to rehearse to the world the story of salvation. As the rite also reminds us, by the very act of eating and drinking we "proclaim the Lord's death until He comes."[9]

---

7 *LSB*, 165.

8 *LSB*, 164.

9 *LSB*, 162.

Post-Communion Collect

Three prayers following the Distribution are provided in *Lutheran Service Book*. The first two offer thanksgiving for the divine gifts that have been received. The third option reminds us that this is "a foretaste of the feast to come."[10] We know that Christ, the Bridegroom, will come to take His Bride—the Church—to that great "feast to come," that great marriage feast of the Lamb. We affirm with the apostle Paul that "for now we see in a mirror dimly, but then face to face. Now I know in part; then I shall know fully, even as I have been fully known" (1 Corinthians 13:12). Paul's affirmation is reflected in that great medieval hymn of the thirteenth century by Thomas Aquinas:

> O Christ, whom now beneath a veil we see,
> May what we thirst for soon our portion be:
> To gaze on Thee unveiled and see Thy face,
> The vision of Thy glory, and Thy grace. (*LSB* 640:5)

To that, we as Christians can only respond: "Amen. Come, Lord Jesus" (Revelation 22:20).

Benediction

Following the Distribution, Post-Communion Canticle, and Post-Communion Collect, the service moves quickly to its conclusion with the Benediction. Just as we began the service by invoking the name of the Holy Trinity, so we leave with the blessing or benediction of that same God—Father, Son, and Holy Spirit—ringing in our ears. It is the so-called Aaronic Blessing (Numbers 6:24–26):

> The Lord bless you and keep you.
> The Lord make His face shine on you and be gracious to you.
> The Lord look upon you with favor and ☩ give you peace.[11]

The congregation responds: "Amen."

---

10 *LSB*, 166.

11 *LSB*, 166.

Having received God's blessing, we go forth, out into the world to witness to that which we have heard and seen and to serve. Having been forgiven, we forgive. Having been accepted, so we accept others. Having been loved without condition, so we love others.

And when the week is over, we return. We come back again to hear and to be fed, to hear the Word and to be nourished once again with Christ's body and blood in Holy Communion, the food we need for our life's journey. With sin forgiven and hearts full and overflowing, we can sing, in the words of Jaroslav J. Vajda's hymn:

> So much to sing about: all I have seen and heard,
> Your glory in my talents' use my best reward:
>   that others see what I have seen
> And sing with me: "It is the Lord!"[12]

With thirst quenched and hunger satisfied, we offer what we have received to the world, that the world might see what we have seen and hear what we have heard.

That, in the final analysis, is what worship is all about.

12 "So Much to Sing About," *Sing Peace, Sing Gift of Peace: The Comprehensive Hymnary of Jaroslav J. Vajda* (St. Louis: Concordia Publishing House, 2003), 210.

Appendix: History of the Development of the Divine Service

The Medieval Mass (ca. 1000)	Luther's Latin Mass (1523)	Luther's German Mass (1526)	The Common Service (1888)
ENTRANCE RITES			
Introit	Introit	Introit (psalm or hymn)	Introit
Kyrie	*Kyrie*	*Kyrie*	*Kyrie*
Gloria in Excelsis	*Gloria in Excelsis*	Collect	*Gloria in Excelsis*
	Collect		Collect
SERVICE OF READINGS			
Epistle	Epistle	Epistle	Epistle
Gradual	Gradual or Alleluia	Gradual hymn	Alleluia
Alleluia or Tract	Gospel	Gospel	Gospel
Sequence (optional)	Nicene Creed	Nicene Creed (metrical version)	Creed
Gospel	Sermon	Sermon	Sermon
Sermon (optional)	Preparation of the Elements		General Prayers
Creed			
Prayers			
SACRIFICE OF THE MASS			
Offertory Rites	Preface and Proper Preface	Paraphrase of Lord's Prayer	*Sanctus* and Hosanna
Eucharistic Prayers	Words of Institution	Words of Institution (*Sanctus*, *Agnus Dei*, or other hymns between divided Words of Institution)	Exhortation to the Communicants
Preface	*Sanctus*		Lord's Prayer and Words of Institution or Words of Institution and Lord's Prayer
Sanctus	Lord's Prayer		*Agnus Dei*
Canon	Pax Domini		Distribution
Lord's Prayer	*Agnus Dei*		
Agnus Dei	Communion hymn		
Communion			
Prayers	Collect	Collect	Collect and Thanksgiving
Post-Communion	*Benedicamus*	Benediction	Benediction
Ite, missa est or *Benedicamus Domino*	Benediction		

Joyful Singing: A Story of Lutheran Sacred Music in Texas.
Benjamin A. Kolodziej

Paul O. Manz: The Enduring Legacy of the Hymn Festival.
James W. Freese

A Small Catechism: Understanding Church Music in the Lutheran Tradition.
Carl Schalk

A Large Catechism: Understanding Church Music in the Lutheran Tradition.
Carl Schalk and Paul Westermeyer

The Choir and the Organ in Early Lutheranism.
Daniel Zager and Steven Wente

Church Music in the United States: 1760–1901.
David W. Music and Paul Westermeyer

Charles W. Ore: An American Original.
Irene Beethe, editor

I Walk with Angels: The Life and Work of James Engel.
Carl R. Ziebell

Anna B. Hoppe: Her Life and Hymnody.
Elisabeth Joy Urtel

Prelude and Fugue on the Life of Harriet Reynolds Krauth Spaeth (1845–1925). Robert D. Hawkins

Dawnlight Breaks: The Hymn Texts and Translations of F. Samuel Janzow.
David W. Rogner

August Crull and the Story of the Evangelical Lutheran Hymn-Book 1912.
Jon D. Vieker

Singing the Church's Song: Essays and Occasional Writings on Church Music. Carl Schalk

The Precious Gift: The Hymns, Carols, and Translations of Henry L. Lettermann. Scott M. Hyslop

Luther Reed: The Legacy of a Gentleman and a Churchman.
Philip H. Pfatteicher